I Love to Draw Cartoons!

Jennifer Lipsey

LARK BOOKS

A Division of Sterling Publishing Co., Inc.
New York

My Very Favorite Art Book

To my son Oliver who shared the same due date as this book.

Editor
JOE RHATIGAN

Creative Director
CELIA NARANJO

Assistant Editor
ROSE MCLARNEY

Art Assistant
BRADLEY NORRIS

Library of Congress Cataloging-in-Publication Data

Lipsey, Jennifer.
  I love to draw cartoons! / Jennifer Lipsey.
    p. cm. -- (My very favorite art book)
  Includes index.
  ISBN-13: 978-1-57990-819-5 (hc-plc with jacket : alk. paper)
  ISBN-10: 1-57990-819-5 (hc-plc with jacket : alk. paper)
  1. Cartooning--Technique--Juvenile literature. 2.
Drawing--Technique--Juvenile literature. I. Title.
  NC1320.L57 2007
  741.5'1--dc22

                          2007004414

10 9 8 7 6 5 4 3 2 1

First Edition

Published by Lark Books, A Division of
Sterling Publishing Co., Inc.
387 Park Avenue South, New York, N.Y. 10016

© 2007, Jennifer Lipsey

Distributed in Canada by Sterling Publishing,
c/o Canadian Manda Group, 165 Dufferin Street
Toronto, Ontario, Canada M6K 3H6

Distributed in the United Kingdom by GMC Distribution Services,
Castle Place, 166 High Street, Lewes, East Sussex, England BN7 1XU

Distributed in Australia by Capricorn Link (Australia) Pty Ltd.,
P.O. Box 704, Windsor, NSW 2756 Australia

If you have questions or comments about this book, please contact:
Lark Books
67 Broadway
Asheville, NC 28801
(828) 253-0467

Manufactured in China

ISBN 13: 978-1-57990-819-5
ISBN 10: 1-57990-819-5

For information about custom editions, special sales, premium and corporate purchases, please contact Sterling Special Sales Department at 800-805-5489 or specialsales@sterlingpub.com.

Contents

Drawing Cartoons Is Fun! • 4

Four Steps to Finishing a Cartoon • 5

Letter Faces • 6

Eyes • 8

Noses • 10

Mouths • 12

Simple People • 14

Poseable People • 16

Superheroes • 18

Circle Animals • 20

Cats • 22

Dogs • 24

Farm Animals • 26

Jungle Animals • 28

Desert Critters • 30

Pond Animals • 32

Dinosaurs • 34

Monsters • 36

Funny Folks • 38

Cars • 40

Buildings • 42

Holidays • 44

Cartoon Words • 46

Index • 48

Drawing Cartoons is FUN!

A cartoon is usually a funny drawing. Sometimes it will tell a story, but it doesn't have to. Drawing takes PRACTICE so be patient with yourself.

Everyone's drawings look different. So don't worry if yours aren't just like the ones in this book.

Have fun practicing drawing cartoons! You may even be inspired to make up some of your own characters.

Here are the 4 steps to finishing a Cartoon:

1. Draw

Follow the steps in this book and use a pencil to draw your cartoon LIGHTLY.

2. Ink

Go over the pencil lines you want to keep with a black pen or marker. This is called "inking."

3. Erase

Erase all the leftover pencil lines.

4. Color

Fill in your cartoon with markers, crayons, colored pencils, or paint. You're done!

Let's Draw Cartoons!

Letter Faces

Letter "U" Face

1.

Draw a capital letter "U."

2.

Draw eyes over the "U."

3.

Add a mouth.

4.

Draw a circle around the face. Add ears if you want.

Letter "Z" Face

1.

Draw a "Z."

2.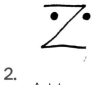

Add eyes.

3.

Draw a mouth and eyebrow.

4.

Draw the head. Try some hair.

Letter G Face

1.

Draw a capital letter "G."

2.

Draw eyes.

3.

Add eyebrows and a mouth.

4.

Draw the head, ears, and hair.

Letter "S" Face

1.   2.   3.   4.

Try different hairstyles.

Make it funny!

Add a body.

Letter "J" Face

1.   2.   3.   4.

7

Eyes

Dot & Line Eyes

Dots   Straight lines   Curved lines

Now put together the dots and lines
to make many more easy-to-draw eyes.

Circle Eyes

Draw two circles.
Add dots in the
middle.

Now move the dots to
make the eyes look in
different directions.

Try different eyebrows.

Expressive Eyes

1.

Draw an oval or
a circle.

2.

Draw another
one next to it.

3.

Add dots for
pupils.

4.

Draw lines for
eyelids.

5.

Add
eyebrows.

Show Different Emotions

 Mad

 Scared

Sleepy

 Crazy

 Sneaky

 Happy

 Sad

It's all in the eyes.

Try thick eyebrows.

I'm an angry bear.

ALL THIS SITTING MAKES ME TIRED.

Draw one of your favorite characters. Leave out the eyes. Make copies of it or trace it. Try out lots of different eyes. See page 21 if you want to draw this bear.

It's amazing how changing the eyes can make your character look totally different.

YOU'RE THE ARTIST. HOW SHOULD I FEEL TODAY?

Noses

Simple "C" Nose

A letter "C" makes a good cartoon nose.

Draw lots of circles for heads. Then try drawing letter "C" noses in different directions. The nose shows where the head is looking. Now add eyes.

Different Nose Sizes

Do you want little, big, long, or fat "C" noses?

More Fun Noses

Try lots of different noses!

Trace these noses for practice if you want.

Draw a face and practice putting noses on it.

People will look like they are having a conversation if their noses face each other.

Yum! Fresh-baked cookies.
Can you draw this boy's nose?

Mouths

One-Line Mouths

Just one line can make lots of different mouths.

Try it!

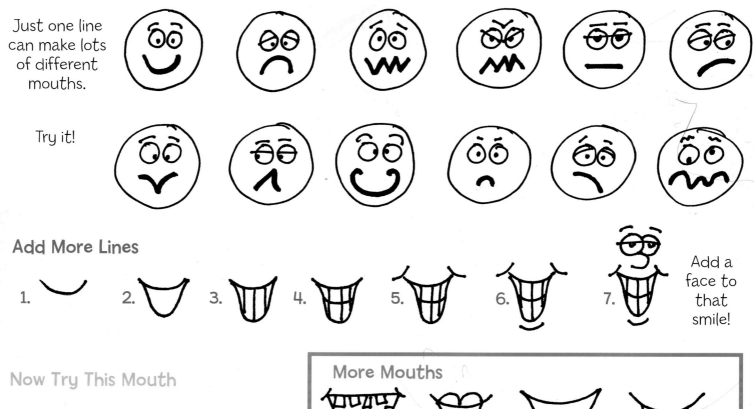

Add More Lines

1. 2. 3. 4. 5. 6. 7.

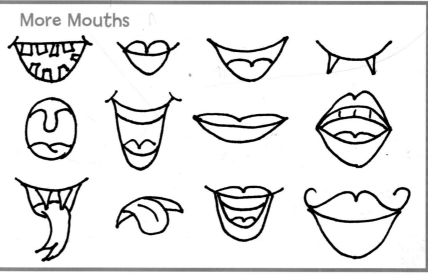

Add a face to that smile!

Now Try This Mouth

1. Draw a curved line.

2. Add another.

3. Draw lips.

4. Add a tongue.

More Mouths

Simple People

Basic Person

1. 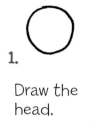 Draw the head.

2. Add the body.

3.  Draw a square with a line in the middle for legs.

4. Add feet.

5. Draw arms and hands.

6. Now draw a face.

Sideways Person

1. Begin with the head and body.

2.  Draw the line between the legs closer to the side your person is looking.

3.  Add three angled lines for shoes.

4.  Draw one line across the bottom of the feet.

5.  An arm fits inside the body. Add a face.

 Why not draw your person facing the other way?

You can use this basic person to make lots of different people.

Practice changing their hair, clothes, and faces.

Have fun with it!

Draw wider and rounder bodies for big people.

Draw more holiday cartoons on page 45.

Try drawing a very small person.

For a dress, make the body lines longer.

To make an astronaut, draw the head bigger and add moon boots.

Curved arms and legs make a cowboy!

Poseable People

1. Draw a circle for a head and a line for the body.

2. Add a line for the shoulders. Draw a shorter line below it for the hips.

3. Now add some arm and leg lines.

4. Feet lines come next.

5. Outline your stick person to draw clothes. Draw simple hands and shoes.

6. Ink it. Erase the extra pencil lines. Add a face, too.

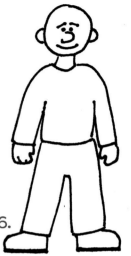

1. Now try drawing different poses.

2. Outline the stick person lines to make clothes and body parts.

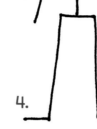

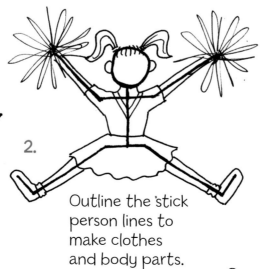

3. Go over the other lines in marker. Erase the stick person lines you drew first. Color it in.

Good job!

When you draw someone from the side, you don't need the hip and shoulder lines.

Your character will look like she is running if you draw both feet off the ground.

Cartoon babies have big heads and small bodies.

Draw a giant with a small head and a big, tall body.

Try adding knee and elbow joints to the stick person.

Small trees make him look big.

Superheroes

Basic Male Superhero

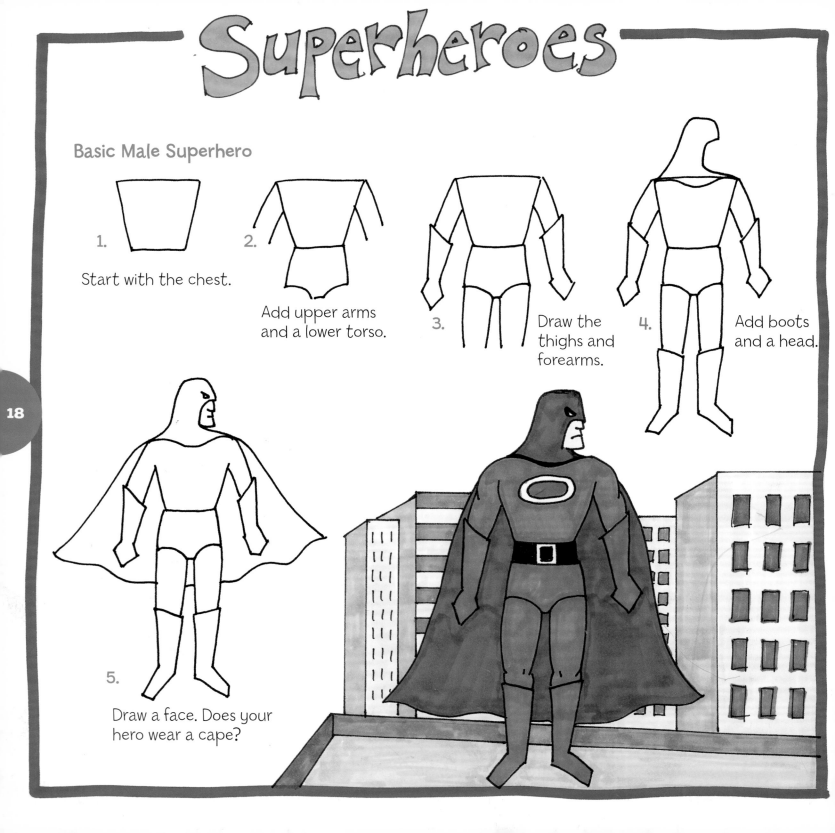

1. Start with the chest.

2. Add upper arms and a lower torso.

3. Draw the thighs and forearms.

4. Add boots and a head.

5. Draw a face. Does your hero wear a cape?

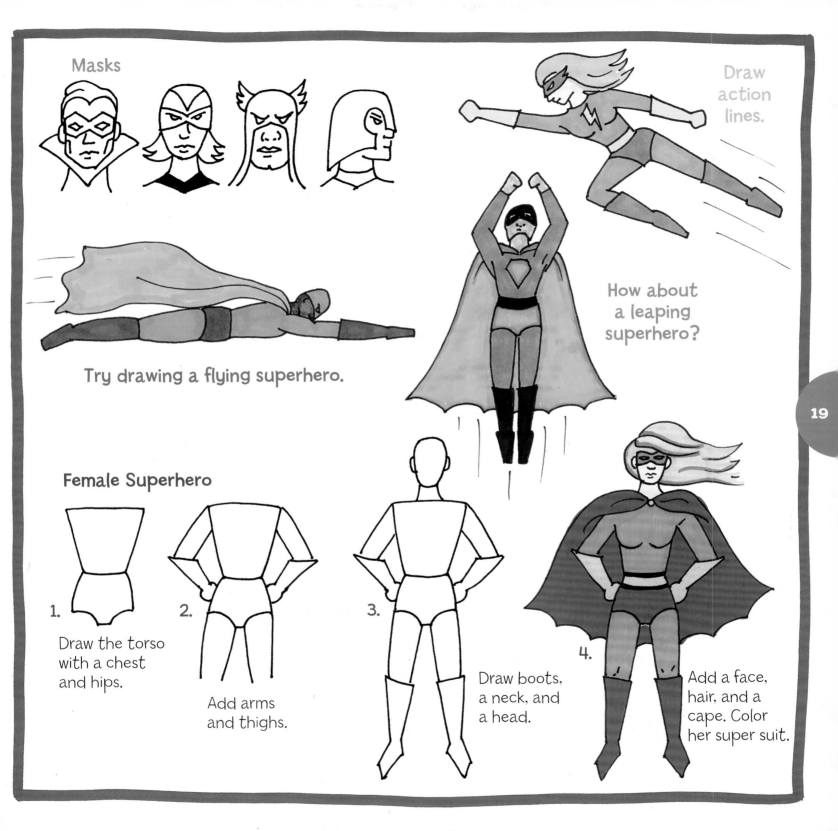

Masks

Draw action lines.

Try drawing a flying superhero.

How about a leaping superhero?

19

Female Superhero

1. Draw the torso with a chest and hips.

2. Add arms and thighs.

3. Draw boots, a neck, and a head.

4. Add a face, hair, and a cape. Color her super suit.

Circle Animals

Panda Bear

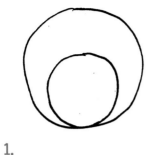

1. Draw a large circle for the body. Draw a smaller circle inside for the head.

2. For ears, draw two half circles on the head. For a snout, add a small circle inside the head.

3. Draw rounded legs starting from the body. Add half circles to the snout for eye patches.

4. Draw eyes, a nose, and a mouth. Color the ears, legs, and eye patches black.

Fat Mouse

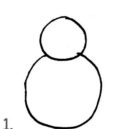

1. Draw a circle head over a circle body.

2. Add big ears and little feet.

3. Draw half circles inside the ears and belly. Add arms.

4. Draw a long, pointy nose. Add eyes and a tail.

Teddy Bear

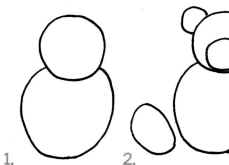

1. Draw a circle head over an oval body.

2. Draw half circle ears and oval feet. Add a circle for the snout.

3. Connect the feet to the body. Draw arms.

4. Draw half circles and ovals inside the feet, belly, and ears.

Bunny Rabbit

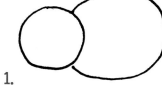

1. Draw a circle head over an oval body.

2. Draw a circle tail and rabbit ears.

3. Draw a curved line for the back leg. Add paws and a face.

Try drawing different eyes. See page 8.

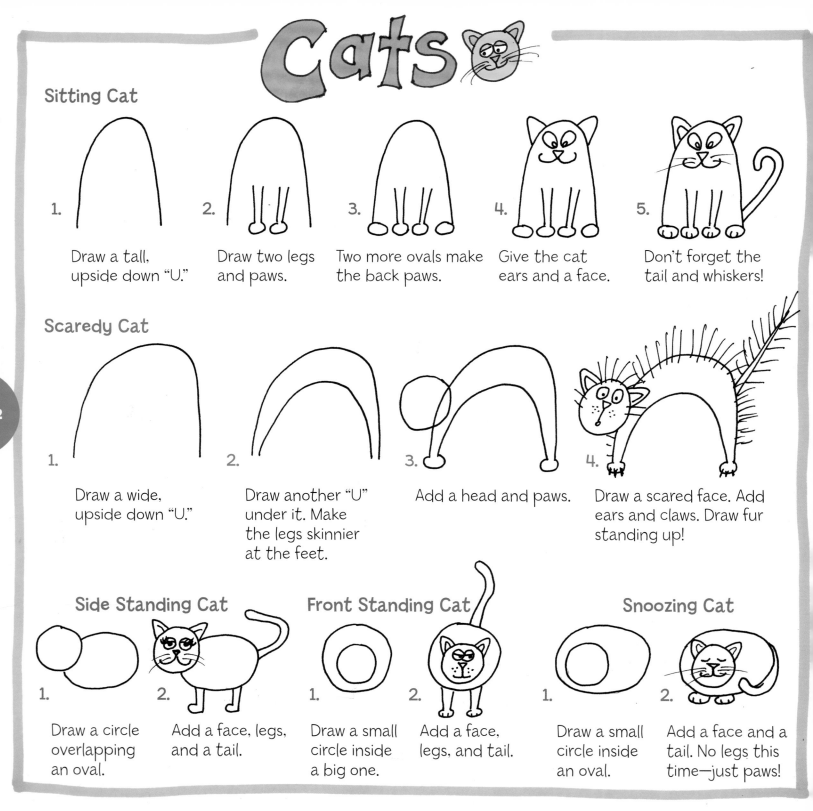

Cats

Sitting Cat

1. Draw a tall, upside down "U."

2. Draw two legs and paws.

3. Two more ovals make the back paws.

4. Give the cat ears and a face.

5. Don't forget the tail and whiskers!

Scaredy Cat

1. Draw a wide, upside down "U."

2. Draw another "U" under it. Make the legs skinnier at the feet.

3. Add a head and paws.

4. Draw a scared face. Add ears and claws. Draw fur standing up!

Side Standing Cat

1. Draw a circle overlapping an oval.

2. Add a face, legs, and a tail.

Front Standing Cat

1. Draw a small circle inside a big one.

2. Add a face, legs, and tail.

Snoozing Cat

1. Draw a small circle inside an oval.

2. Add a face and a tail. No legs this time—just paws!

A fat cat has a big
body and a small head!

Could your scaredy cat be
a stretching cat instead?

Yikes! A scaredy cat needs
big, surprised eyes.

KEEP OUT!

Dogs

Sitting Dog

1. Draw a tall, curved line. Add two leg lines.

2. Add the front paws.

3. Don't forget the back legs.

4. Give him some floppy ears.

5. Draw a face, tail, a belly line, and other details.

Standing Dog

1. Draw the head.

2. Add the body.

3. Draw four legs.

4. Add ears and a tail.

5. Your puppy needs a face.

Short Dog

1. Draw the head and snout.

2. A long oval forms the body.

3. Add some short legs.

4. Draw a long ear.

5. Add a tail and face.

Shaggy Dog

1. Draw rounded blocks for the head and body.

2. Add legs, ears, and a tail.

3. Short, squiggly lines make great shaggy fur.

4. Add eyes, a mouth, and more fur. Erase the pencil lines.

Try making up your own dog.

Your dog can be any color or have any pattern you want.

Farm Animals

Sheep

1. Draw a fluffy cloud shape.

2. For the head, draw a letter "U." Add eyes on top.

3. Draw a fluffy head and tail.

4. Add some ears and some "d"-shaped legs.

Cow

1. Draw a rounded head and body.

2. Add legs and ears.

3. Draw the udder, tail, and horns.

4. Finish with a funny face, spots, and small lines for hooves.

Duck

1. Draw a curved body and short neck.

2. Add a head, tail, and legs.

3. Draw the bill. Then add paddle feet.

4. How about some funny eyes? Then draw a wing.

Horse

1. Draw a rounded body and two lines for the neck.

2. Add a head and legs.

3. Draw a mouth, ears, and hooves.

4. Add a face, tail, and mane.

Pig

1.

2.

1.

2.

How about an amazing jumping horse?

Try drawing a duck in water.

Make your animals any color you want.

Jungle Animals

Tiger

1. Draw a head.

2. Add a rounded body.

3. Attach some legs to the body. Draw semicircle ears on the head.

4. Add a face, tail, and stripes.

Elephant

1. Draw a circle for the head.

2. Add an oval body.

3. Draw a big ear and thick legs.

4. Add a trunk, tail, eye, and toenails.

Giraffe

1. Start with the body and legs.

2. Add a long neck.

3. Draw an oval head and a small tail.

4. Your giraffe needs a face, horns, an ear, and spots.

Ink it. Erase the extra pencil lines.

Color it!

28

How about a baby elephant?

What other jungle animals can you think of?

Front Facing Animals

1.

2.

1.

2.

To make a lion, draw a tiger shape but forget the stripes. Add a mane instead!

Desert Critters

Rattlesnake

1. Draw the bottom coil and the head.

2. Add more coils.

3. The tail and rattle go at the top of the coil.

4. Draw the snake's face. Add some markings, too.

Scorpion

1. Start with an oval body.

2. Add the front arms and claws.

3. The tail and a stinger are next.

4. Don't forget the face and legs.

Tarantula

1. Draw the head and body.

2. Draw eight curved leg lines.

3. To make thick legs, connect the lines back around to the body.

4. Draw a bunch of eyes. Add lots of little hairs.

Gila Monster

1. Draw the body and head.

2. Add a thick tail, legs, and claws.

3. Draw a face. Then add tail stripes and a pattern on the body.

Pond Animals

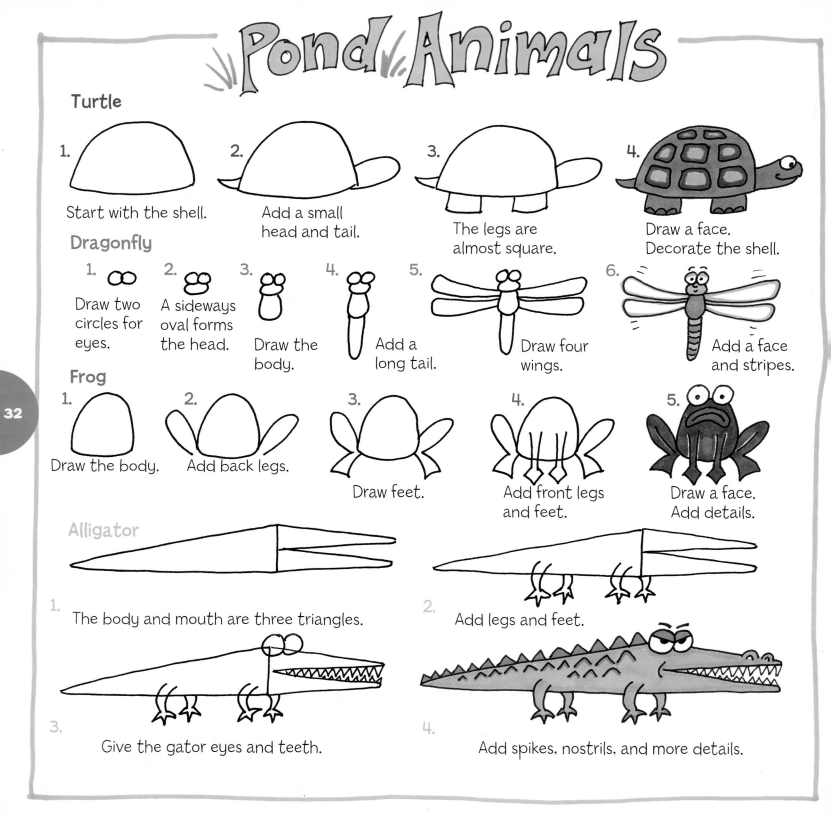

Turtle

1. Start with the shell.
2. Add a small head and tail.
3. The legs are almost square.
4. Draw a face. Decorate the shell.

Dragonfly

1. Draw two circles for eyes.
2. A sideways oval forms the head.
3. Draw the body.
4. Add a long tail.
5. Draw four wings.
6. Add a face and stripes.

Frog

1. Draw the body.
2. Add back legs.
3. Draw feet.
4. Add front legs and feet.
5. Draw a face. Add details.

Alligator

1. The body and mouth are three triangles.
2. Add legs and feet.
3. Give the gator eyes and teeth.
4. Add spikes, nostrils, and more details.

Dinosaurs

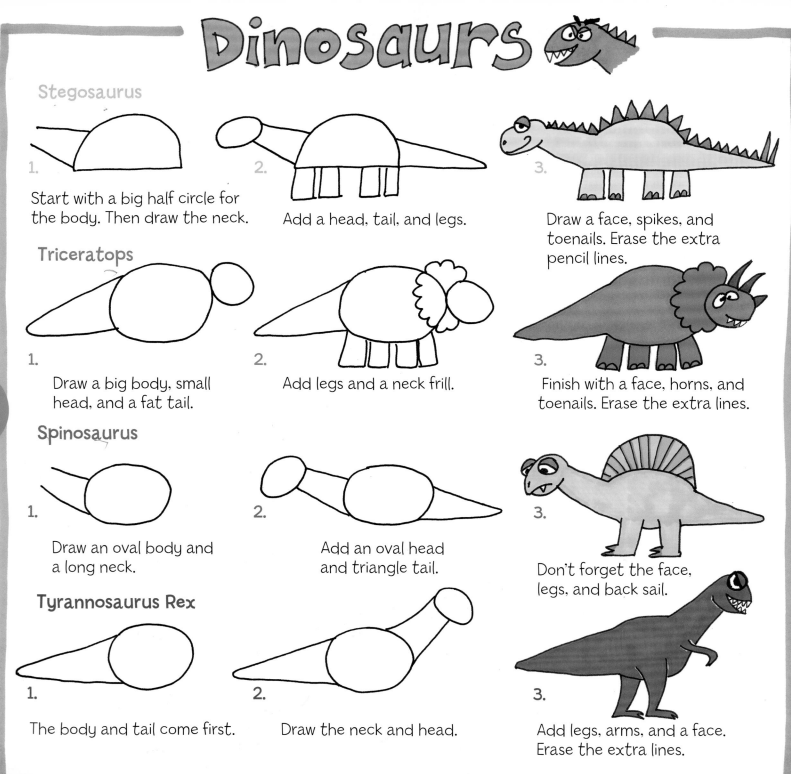

Stegosaurus

1. Start with a big half circle for the body. Then draw the neck.

2. Add a head, tail, and legs.

3. Draw a face, spikes, and toenails. Erase the extra pencil lines.

Triceratops

1. Draw a big body, small head, and a fat tail.

2. Add legs and a neck frill.

3. Finish with a face, horns, and toenails. Erase the extra lines.

Spinosaurus

1. Draw an oval body and a long neck.

2. Add an oval head and triangle tail.

3. Don't forget the face, legs, and back sail.

Tyrannosaurus Rex

1. The body and tail come first.

2. Draw the neck and head.

3. Add legs, arms, and a face. Erase the extra lines.

Try making up your own funny dinosaur.

Don't forget to name it. Let's call this one a Stilt-o-saurus!

WANTED
DEAD OR ALIVE

Your dinosaur characters could wear clothes, too!

Front Facing Dinosaur

1.

Draw the head inside the body.

2.

Add legs, a tail, and a face.

Draw small trees to show how big your dinosaur is.

Monsters

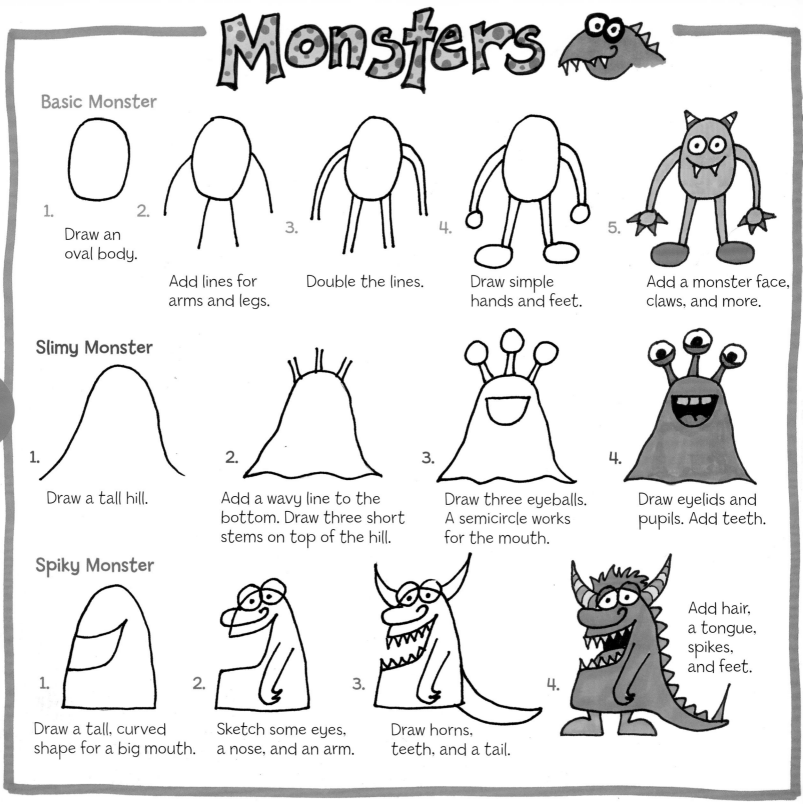

Basic Monster

1. Draw an oval body.

2. Add lines for arms and legs.

3. Double the lines.

4. Draw simple hands and feet.

5. Add a monster face, claws, and more.

Slimy Monster

1. Draw a tall hill.

2. Add a wavy line to the bottom. Draw three short stems on top of the hill.

3. Draw three eyeballs. A semicircle works for the mouth.

4. Draw eyelids and pupils. Add teeth.

Spiky Monster

1. Draw a tall, curved shape for a big mouth.

2. Sketch some eyes, a nose, and an arm.

3. Draw horns, teeth, and a tail.

4. Add hair, a tongue, spikes, and feet.

Funny Folks

Pizza Man

1.

Draw something simple. How about a pizza slice?

2.

Give it a face.

3.

Try adding arms, legs, or both.

4.

If you want, write a caption.

You can make plants walk and talk, too.

How about some flower friends?

Try a branch boy.

Cars

Little Car

1.

Use straight lines to draw the body.

2.

Add the roof and wheel wells.

3.

Now for some tires and bumpers.

4.

Draw windows, headlights, and other details.

Try putting people or animals in your car.

Where is your car going? What is the weather like?

Old Convertible

1.

Start with a long body that's rounded on one side.

2.

Add wheel wells and a windshield.

3.

Draw tires, headlights, and more details.

Superhero Car

1. Start with a long, thin body.

2. Draw a large fin.

3. Add tires and a bubble on top.

Give your car a cool paint job. How about some flames?

Four-Wheel Drive

1. Make a rectangular body with wheel wells.

2. Draw a roof and bumpers.

3. Don't forget windows, a spare tire, a roof rack, and other details.

More Ideas

Try drawing a car from the front.

Give it a face.

It's your car—go anywhere you want.

Have fun!

Buildings

Castle

1. Draw the castle base.

2. Make three towers.

3. Add more towers. Draw triangles on top of each one.

Finish the castle with flags and windows. Draw bricks and add a moat if you want.

School

1. Start with the main building.

2. Add sides to the building. Draw doors, too.

3. Draw windows and a roof.

Add bushes, stairs, and anything else you want.

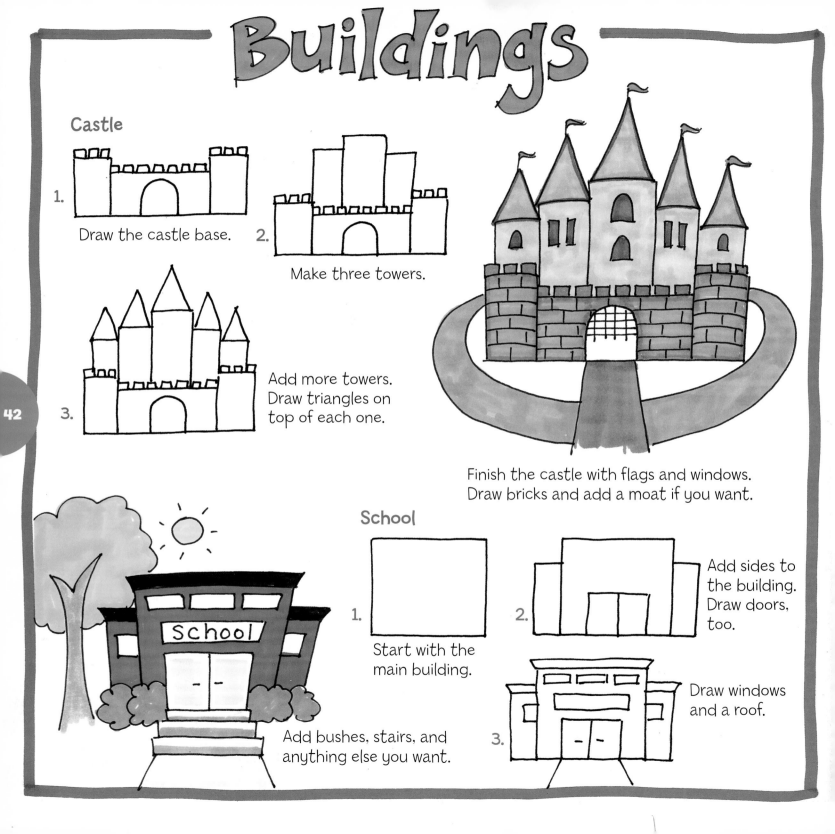

City   Draw a horizontal line. Put different sizes of buildings on it.

1.

2.

Draw more buildings behind them.

Try adding even more buildings. Add details such as windows, smokestacks, and antennas.

Palace

1.

Draw a rectangular base with three rectangles on top.

2.

Add two smaller rectangles.

3.

Draw some tall, skinny towers.

Add windows, turrets, circles, and any other details you can imagine.

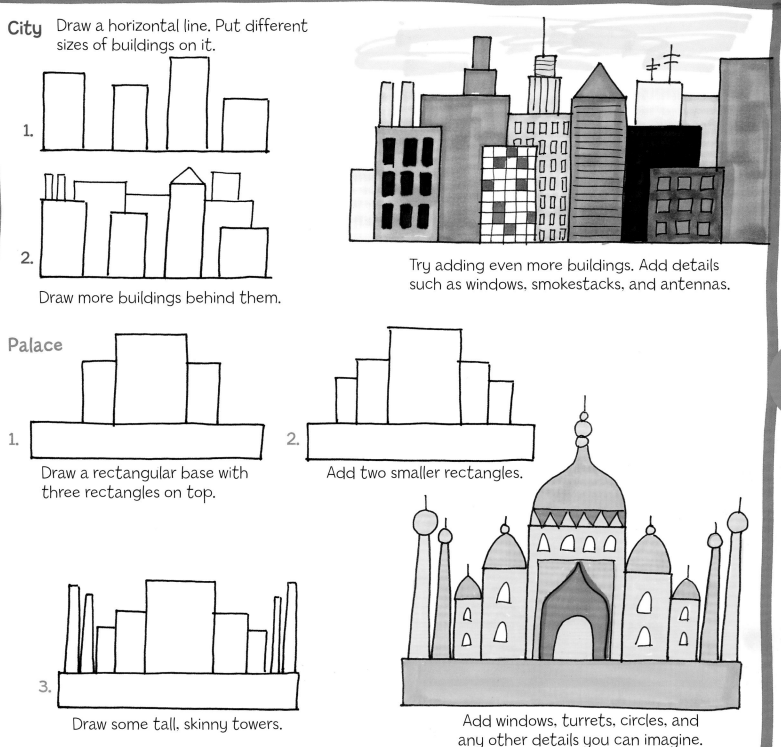

Holidays

Easter Bunny

1. Draw the head with an oval and a half circle.

2. Add the body lines.

3. Draw a middle line to make legs and a curved line to finish the body. Add long feet.

4. Draw arms and floppy ears.

5. Add a face and more details.

Mummy

1. Draw a stick person.

2. Outline it.

3. Add cloth strips. Erase your pencil lines.

Reindeer

1. Draw a body and neck.

2. Add a head and ears.

3. Draw legs and hooves.

4. Add a tail, face, and antlers.

Snowman

1. Start with a snowball head.

2. Draw the second snowball under the first.

3. Add a third snowball. Don't forget a face and stick arms!

Nice boots!

How about a Christmas tree?

Cartoon Words

Bubble Letters

1.

Use a pencil to write a word neatly. Leave a little space between the letters.

2.

Trace around each letter with a curvy line.

3.

Erase the leftover pencil lines.

Comic Book Letters

1.

Lightly draw a curved line in pencil.

2.

Neatly write an action word on the line in capital letters. Leave space between the letters.

3.

Trace around each letter. Draw straight lines where a letter is straight. Draw curved lines where a letter is curvy.

4.

Draw a zigzag around the word. Erase the pencil lines.

Rex

Add bumps to bubble letters to make cloud words.

WHACK!

BANG

Try drawing tall, skinny letters or short, fat letters.

Make your own sign.

STAY OUT!

Try overlapping your bubble letters.

Jennifer

Acknowledgments

I would like to thank the Great Creator, who not only helped me finish my fifth book, but also create and birth a new life.

I am thankful to the hard working folks at Lark Books and to my ever-patient editor, Joe. Even through anxious dreams that I had the baby before completing the work, he always had a warm smile for me.

There are too many friends, family, teachers, students, and parents to thank them all. But please know I truly appreciate your kindness, encouraging words, good advice, and faith in my abilities.

Special thanks to the new daddy, my loving husband, Martin, who took extra good care of his crazy, pregnant wife as she finished her master's degree, a book, and a baby. I love you.

48

Index

Alligator, 32

Basic monster, 36
Basic person, 14
Bubble letters, 46
Bunny rabbit, 21

Castle, 42
City, 43
Comic book letters, 46
Cow, 26

Dot and line eyes, 8
Dragonfly, 32
Duck, 26

Easter bunny, 44
Expressive eyes, 8

Fat mouse, 20
Female superhero, 19
Finishing a cartoon, 5
Four-wheel drive, 41
Frog, 32
Front facing animals, 29
Front facing car, 41
Front facing dinosaur, 35

Gila monster, 30

Horse, 26

Introduction, 4-5

Little car, 40

Male superhero, 18
Mummy, 44

Old convertible, 40
One-line mouths, 12

Palace, 43
Panda bear, 20
Pig, 27

Rattlesnake, 30
Reindeer, 45

Scaredy cat, 22
School, 42
Scorpion, 30
Shaggy dog, 24
Sheep, 26
Short dog, 24
Side standing cat, 22
Sideways person, 14
Sitting cat, 22
Sitting dog, 24
Slimy monster, 36
Snowman, 45
Spiky monster, 36
Spinosaurus, 34
Standing dog, 24
Stegosaurus, 34
Superhero car, 41

Tarantula, 30
Teddy bear, 21
Triceratops, 34
Turtle, 32
Tyrannosaurus Rex, 34